CHRISTIANITY

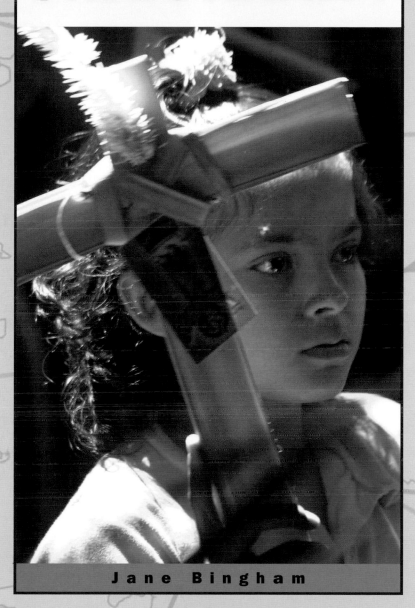

Jane Bingham

W

FRANKLIN WATTS
LONDON • SYDNEY

First published in 2007 by Franklin Watts

© 2007 Arcturus Publishing Limited

Franklin Watts
338 Euston Road
London NW1 3BH

Franklin Watts Australia
Level 17/207 Kent St, Sydney, NSW 2000

Produced by Arcturus Publishing Limited,
26/27 Bickels Yard, 151–153 Bermondsey Street, London
SE1 3HA

Series concept: Alex Woolf
Editor and picture researcher: Alex Woolf
Designer: Simon Borrough
Cartography: Encompass Graphics
Consultant: Douglas G Heming

Picture credits:
Art Archive: 17 (Jan Vinchon Numismatist, Paris/Dagli
Orti), 23 (Abbey of Monteoliveto Maggiore Siena/Dagli
Orti [A]), 25 (British Library), 33.
Corbis: cover (Oswaldo Rivas/Reuters), 5 (Gianni Dagli
Orti), 6 (Brooklyn Museum), 9 (National Gallery,
London), 10 (Archivo Iconográfico, S.A.), 12–13 (Eric
and David Hosking), 15 (Archivo Iconográfico, S.A.), 18
(Archivo Iconográfico, S.A.), 21 (David Samuel
Robbins), 27 (Archivo Iconográfico, S.A.), 28 (James L.
Amos), 31 (Eric Crichton), 35 (Bettmann), 36
(Underwood & Underwood), 39 (Bettmann), 40 (You
Sung-Ho/Reuters).

Cover picture:
A Catholic girl during a mass on Palm Sunday, 2005, in
the Metropolitan Cathedral in Managua, Nicaragua.

A CIP catalogue record for this book is available from
the British Library

Dewey Decimal Classification Number: 230

ISBN: 978 0 7496 6975 1

Printed in China

Franklin Watts is a division of Hachette Children's Books.

CONTENTS

CHAPTER 1: THE LIFE OF JESUS

The Christian religion began with the life of Jesus of Nazareth in the first century CE. Christians believe that Jesus is the Son of God. They teach that Jesus came to Earth to save people from their sins and to show them how to live holy lives, following God's commandments. Jesus spent all his life in Palestine, in the Middle East. Christians often call the region where Jesus lived the 'Holy Land'. Most of this area is now in the modern State of Israel.

Jesus was born around the year 4 CE in the kingdom of Judea. This was the ancient land of the Jews, but by the time of Jesus' birth, it was part of the Roman Empire. The emperor Augustus ruled the empire, but he allowed a local ruler, King Herod, to run Judea according to Roman laws. Herod ruled from 37 BCE to 4 CE.

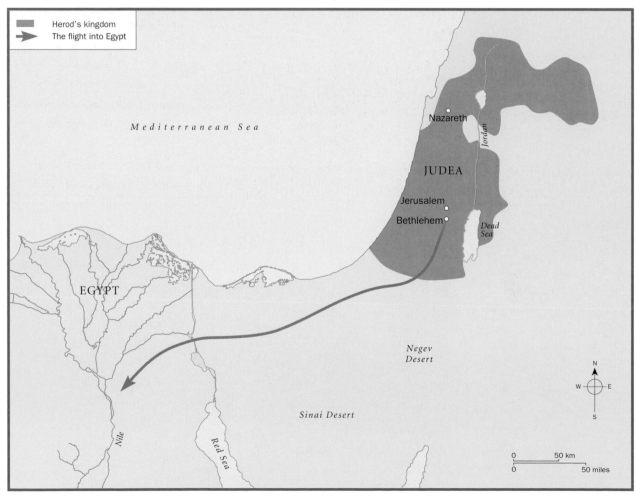

King Herod's kingdom at the time of the birth of Jesus. This map also shows the route that the holy family took when they escaped from Judea into Egypt.

According to the Bible, the first people to visit the baby Jesus were some local shepherds. They were told about Jesus' birth by an angel and they brought lambs as gifts for him. This painting, called the *Adoration of the Shepherds*, is by the 17th-century Spanish artist, Bartolomé Murillo.

The birth of Jesus The story of Jesus' birth is told in the Bible (see panel). It begins with the Annunciation, when the Angel Gabriel appeared to a woman called Mary (known to Christians as the Virgin Mary) to tell her she would give birth to the Son of God. The Annunciation took place at Mary's home in the village of Nazareth, in a hilly northern region of Palestine known as Galilee.

Just before Jesus was born, Mary and her husband Joseph set off on a journey to Joseph's home town of Bethlehem, 160 kilometres to the south. They had to make this journey because Emperor Augustus had decreed that everyone in the Roman Empire had to return to their birthplace to be registered. The Bible tells how Jesus was born in a stable in Bethlehem, because all the inns in the town were full.

The flight into Egypt

Some time after Jesus was born, three wise men arrived to worship the baby Jesus. According to the Bible, they had travelled from countries in the east, following a very bright star. But before they reached Bethlehem, the wise men visited King Herod in Jerusalem to ask about the newborn king. The news of Jesus' birth made Herod very jealous and he ordered that all the baby boys in his kingdom should be murdered.

Herod's plan to kill the baby Jesus did not succeed. Joseph had been warned by an angel in a dream, so he left Bethlehem and travelled with his family to Egypt. This long and difficult journey involved crossing the Negev and Sinai deserts. Christians call this journey the 'Flight into Egypt' (see map on page 4).

THE BIBLE

The Bible is divided into two main sections. The Old Testament tells the history of the Jews; the New Testament describes the life of Jesus and how his followers spread the Christian faith. The New Testament includes four books, known as the Gospels, which tell the story of the life of Jesus. Each Gospel gives a slightly different version of his life. The writers of the Gospels are Matthew, Mark, Luke and John.

Wherever Jesus travelled, he performed miracles and attracted many followers. Here, Jesus is shown outside the Temple in Jerusalem, curing a man of his disability, while the temple priests look on suspiciously.

The life and works of Jesus

Jesus and his family stayed in Egypt until Herod died and it was safe to return to Nazareth. Jesus spent his childhood in Nazareth, where Joseph taught him the trade of carpentry. Sometimes his family visited Jerusalem for important Jewish festivals.

Most of the events in Jesus' adult life took place around the Sea of Galilee, a large freshwater lake on the River Jordan. In this mountainous area, Jesus travelled from place to place, teaching, healing the sick and performing miracles. He began to attract followers, known as disciples.

On the banks of the Sea of Galilee, Jesus called his first disciples to leave their fishing nets and follow him. St Matthew's Gospel also tells how Jesus caused a storm on the lake to stop, and how he walked on the waters of the Sea of Galilee.

One of Jesus' most famous miracles took place at Bethsaida, on the shores of the Sea of Galilee. Here, Jesus turned five loaves and two fishes into enough food to feed a crowd of 5,000 people. Across the lake, in Capernaum, Jesus performed several miracle cures, while further to the west, in the town of Cana, he turned water into wine at a wedding feast.

Jesus preached wherever he went, but his most famous teaching was the Sermon on the Mount. Archaeologists believe that Jesus gave this sermon on a hill close to Capernaum, overlooking the Sea of Galilee. Today, this hill is known as the Mount of the Beatitudes.

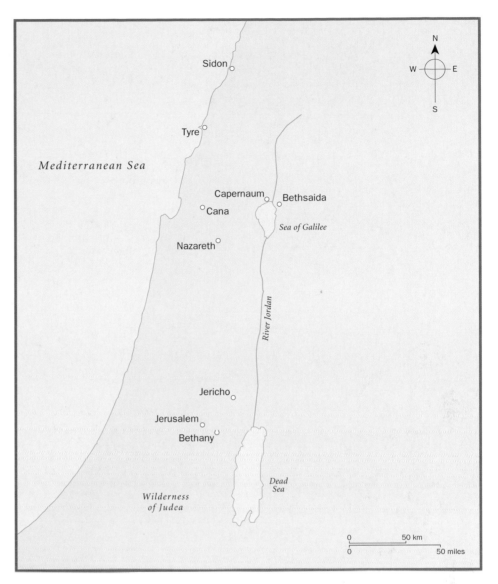

A map of Palestine, showing some of the places where Jesus preached. Jesus spent most of his time around the Sea of Galilee, but he also travelled as far north as Sidon and as far south as Bethany.

JESUS IN THE WILDERNESS

Before he began his work as a preacher, Jesus spent 40 days and 40 nights in the harsh, rocky wilderness of Judea, to the south of Jerusalem. There he struggled with many temptations. According to St Matthew's Gospel, the Devil tempted Jesus to give up his holy way of life in exchange for a life of comfort, power and riches. But Jesus refused all these temptations. Every year, Christians remember Jesus' time in the wilderness in the season of Lent. This season comes directly before Easter and lasts for 40 days.

Jesus' travels The Bible describes several journeys that Jesus took with his disciples. He travelled as far north as the ports of Tyre and Sidon, and as far south as Jerusalem. Jesus also spent some time in Bethany, a village close to Jerusalem. This was the home of his friends Mary and Martha and their brother Lazarus. The Gospel of Saint John tells how Lazarus fell ill and died and then Jesus miraculously brought brought him back to life.

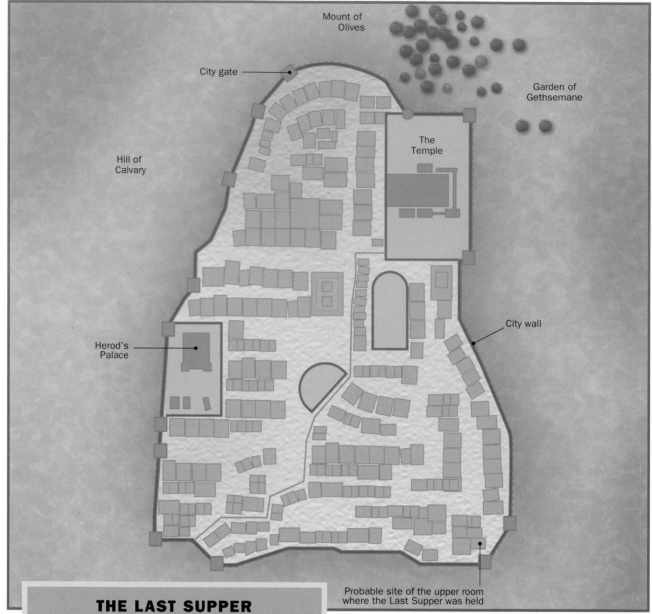

Mount of
Olives

City gate

Garden of
Gethsemane

Hill of
Calvary

The
Temple

City wall

Herod's
Palace

Probable site of the upper room
where the Last Supper was held

THE LAST SUPPER

Not long before he was arrested, Jesus shared a
special meal with all his disciples. This meal,
which became known as the Last Supper, was held
in the upper room of a house in the city. At the
Last Supper, Jesus taught his followers to share
bread and wine in memory of him. He explained
that the bread and wine symbolized his body and
blood. This was the start of the service of Holy
Communion, which is practised by all Christians.
Holy Communion is also known as the Eucharist
and the Mass.

**A plan of Jerusalem, showing some of the places
associated with the last few weeks of Jesus' life.**

In the last weeks of his life, Jesus travelled to Jerusalem.
When he reached a hill called the Mount of Olives near
Jerusalem, Jesus sent two disciples to find a donkey so
that he could ride into the city. The people of Jerusalem
welcomed Jesus. They sang songs and cut down
branches from palm trees to lay in his path.

Preaching and arrest For the next few
weeks, Jesus preached in Jerusalem and cured the sick.
People flocked to see him, praising him as the Son of

God. This made the chief priests very unhappy, especially when Jesus taught in their Temple.

Eventually the priests decided to take action. They persuaded one of the disciples, Judas Iscariot, to betray Jesus. One evening, Judas led a group of soldiers to the Garden of Gethsemane, on the slopes of the Mount of Olives. Jesus was walking in the garden when Judas approached him and gave him a kiss. This was a sign for the soldiers to arrest Jesus.

Crucifixion and Resurrection

Jesus was put on trial by the priests and then passed to Pontius Pilate, the Roman governor of Judea, for sentencing. The priests wanted Pilate to order Jesus' execution. However, Pilate could find no reason to put Jesus to death, so he asked the crowd to choose who should be crucified – Jesus or a thief named Barabas.

By this time, the crowd had turned against Jesus, and they decided that *he* should be crucified. Jesus was given a crown of thorns and forced to carry his heavy wooden cross to a hill called Calvary, just outside the city walls. There, he was crucified between two thieves. Calvary is sometimes also known as Golgotha, which means 'the place of the skull'.

The body of Jesus was buried in a tomb cut out of a rock face, and the tomb was sealed with a heavy stone. However, three days later, Mary Magdalene discovered that the stone had been rolled to one side and the tomb was empty. She was afraid that Jesus' body had been stolen, but the Bible tells that Jesus appeared to her and told her he would soon be with his Father in heaven. This 'rising from the dead' is known as the Resurrection.

The Crucifixion has been painted by many leading Christian artists. This painting is by the Italian artist Raphael (1483–1520). It is called *The Crucified Christ with the Virgin Mary, Saints and Angels*.

CHAPTER 2: SPREADING THE WORD

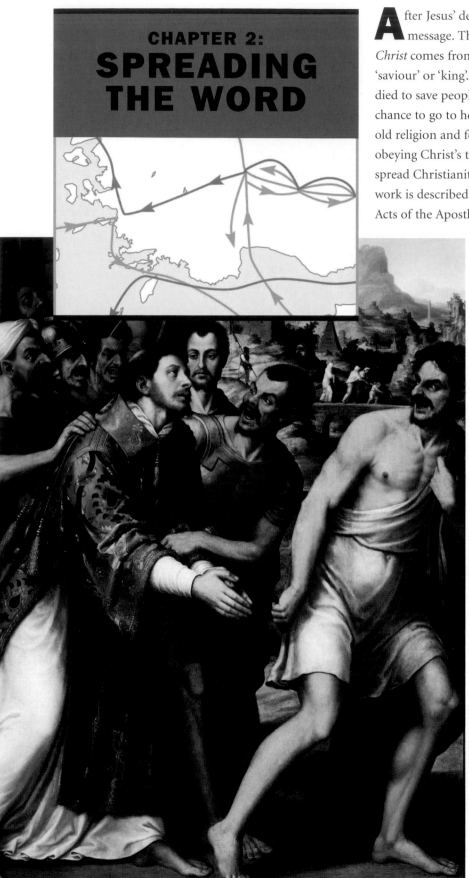

After Jesus' death, his disciples began to spread his message. They referred to him as Jesus Christ. *Christ* comes from the Greek word *christos*, meaning 'saviour' or 'king'. The disciples taught that Christ had died to save people from their sins and to give them the chance to go to heaven. They told people to give up their old religion and follow Christ, and to live a virtuous life obeying Christ's teachings. The followers of Christ who spread Christianity are known as the apostles. Their work is described in a New Testament book called the Acts of the Apostles.

Pentecost The Acts of the Apostles describes how the Holy Spirit appeared to the apostles and gave them inspiration to carry out their work (see panel for more about the Holy Spirit). About two months after the death of Jesus, the

THE TRINITY

Christians believe that God has three forms: God the Father; God the Son; and God the Holy Spirit. Together, all these forms of God are known as the Trinity. God the Son is Jesus Christ. God the Holy Spirit is also often known as the Holy Ghost. In Christian art, the Holy Spirit is sometimes shown as a flame and sometimes takes the form of a white dove.

The martyrdom of Saint Stephen, as seen through the eyes of a 16th-century Spanish artist. Stephen is surrounded by tormenters who are eagerly leading him on to his death.

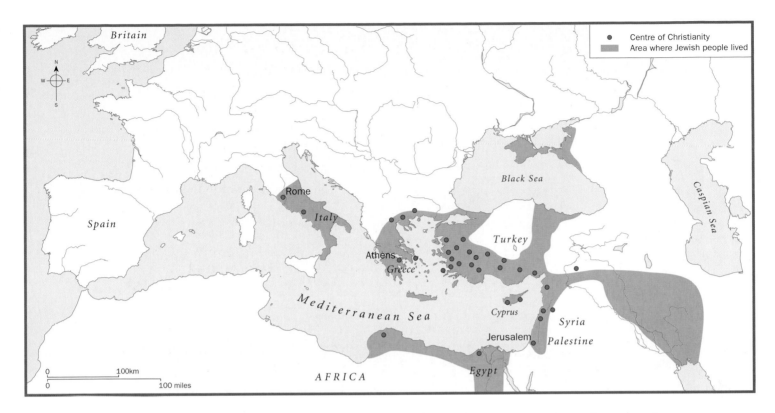

This map shows the main Christian centres at the end of the first century CE. It also shows the areas where Jewish people lived. At this period, most of the converts to Christianity were originally Jews.

apostles met in Jerusalem to celebrate the Jewish harvest festival known as Pentecost. Suddenly, they heard the sound of a powerful wind. Then they saw a flame flickering over each of their heads – a sign that the Holy Spirit was with them.

The apostles realized that they were able to speak in many different languages. They went out into the crowds and began to preach. At that time, Jerusalem was full of Jews who had come from many different lands to celebrate Pentecost. The apostles spoke to them all in their own languages, and told them about Jesus' message.

The message spreads

Gradually, the message of Christianity spread to all the areas of the world where Jewish people lived (see map). At the same time, the apostles began to travel and spread the word. Small communities of Christians became established all over the Middle East. At first, only Jews converted to Christianity, but slowly Christianity spread to gentiles (non-Jews) as well.

Dying for their faith

The apostles made many enemies as they spread their new religion. In particular, the leaders of the Jews, known as the elders, were very angry that their people were abandoning their Jewish faith. Some of the apostles were put to death for preaching Christianity and opposing the commands of the elders. Stephen was stoned to death outside the walls of Jerusalem, while Peter was thrown into the city prison, and later sentenced to death.

People who die for their faith are known as martyrs. Steven and Peter were among the first of many Christian martyrs. After their deaths, they became known as Saint Stephen and Saint Peter. *Saint* (oftened shortened to *St*) is the title given to holy people in the Christian religion.

The conversion of Saul

One of the most important figures in the early history of Christianity is St Paul. But Paul did not start his life as a Christian. As a young man he was named Saul, and he took part in the Jewish persecution of the Christians. He even joined in the stoning of Stephen.

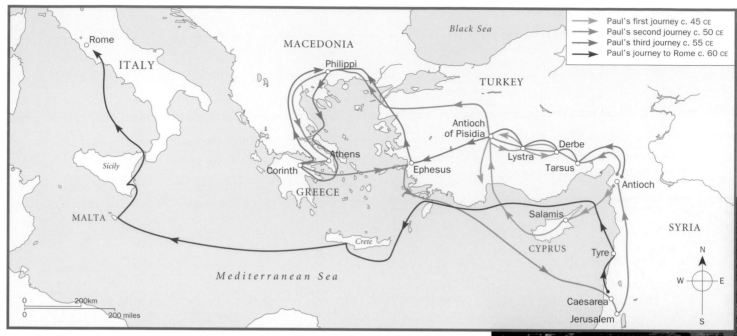

The journeys of Saint Paul. For 25 years, Paul undertook tiring and dangerous journeys over land and sea.

The Acts of the Apostles describes how Saul was converted to Christianity on the road from Jerusalem to Damascus in northern Palestine. As he approached Damascus, Saul had a vision of brilliant light, which left him blind for three days. After he had recovered his sight, Saul became a Christian and changed his name to Paul. He spent the rest of his life travelling, spreading the Christian message.

Paul's first journey

On Paul's first journey, he travelled around the lands of the eastern Mediterranean. First he went to the island of Cyprus and set up a church in Salamis. Then he returned to the mainland and journeyed around the areas that are now Syria and Turkey. In some places, such as Lystra, Paul was welcomed. But in others he was driven away.

Paul's second and third journeys

On his second journey, Paul set off overland to the cities of Tarsus, Lystra and Antioch (in present-day Turkey). Then he crossed the sea to Philippi (in Macedonia), Athens and Corinth (in Greece), and Ephesus (in Turkey). In all these places, Paul set up new communities of Christians.

On his third journey, Paul revisited some of the places he had been to before. While he was in Ephesus, he tried to prevent people from worshipping the goddess Artemis (also known as Diana). This made many people very angry.

Paul's last journey

Paul was arrested when he returned to Jerusalem to visit the Christians there. The Roman rulers in Jerusalem sent him to Rome to be

tried by the emperor. Paul travelled under guard in a merchant ship, which was wrecked off the coast of Malta.

When he finally reached Rome, Paul was arrested. He was allowed to stay in a house, but he had a guard watching him all the time. During this time, Paul continued to preach and wrote many letters (see panel). Nobody is sure how he died, but he may have been beheaded on the orders of Emperor Nero.

PAUL'S LETTERS

While he was travelling, Paul wrote letters to the Christian communities he had set up. These letters encouraged the new Christians in their faith and taught them more about their religion. Later, Paul's letters were included in the New Testament.

Perhaps the most famous of all Paul's letters are his Letters to the Corinthians. They include a well-known passage about love. In this passage, Paul explains that Christians should love each other and all other people. 'Above all remember that without love you are nothing.'

The ancient theatre at Ephesus in Turkey was the scene of a riot against St Paul. Some worshippers of the goddess Diana organized a protest against Paul's teachings, but fortunately the crowd was kept under control.

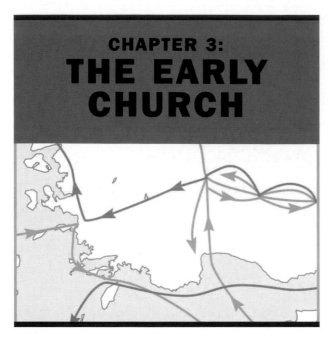

CHAPTER 3: THE EARLY CHURCH

The early Christians met secretly in believers' houses. They usually met on a Sunday, early in the morning or in the evening. The Christians prayed together, sang hymns (songs praising God) and studied the scriptures (the books of the New Testament). They also celebrated Holy Communion, as a reminder of Christ's Last Supper and his death and resurrection. (See panel on the Last Supper on page 8.)

Terrible punishments Some Roman emperors saw Christianity as a serious threat to their power. They took very harsh measures to try to wipe out the new religion. In 64 CE, Emperor Nero blamed the Christians for the Great Fire of Rome. Some Christians were thrown to the dogs, wrapped in animal skins, while others were used as human torches to light up the emperor's parties. Nero also turned the killing of Christians into public entertainment. From this time onwards, Christians were sent into the arenas of public amphitheatres, to be attacked and eaten by lions.

By the end of the first century CE, Christianity was flourishing in many parts of the Roman Empire. The new faith was especially popular in Rome, but many powerful Romans were suspicious of Christianity, so most early Christians did not reveal their faith.

Other Roman emperors had Christians arrested, tortured and killed, but Emperor Diocletian carried out

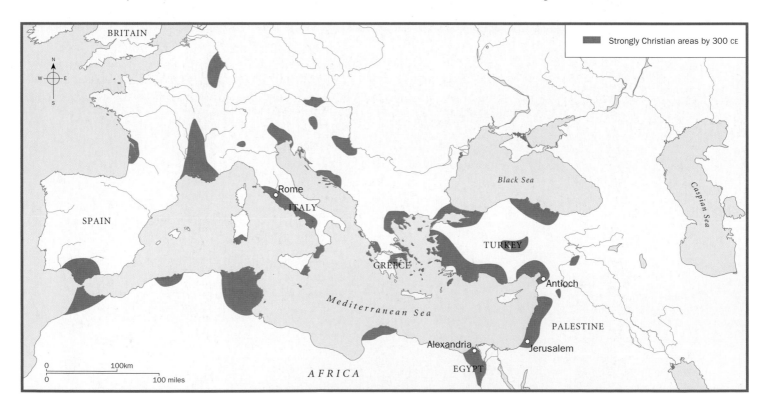

By the end of the third century there were Christian communities all around the Mediterranean Sea. Christianity had also reached parts of northern Europe along the routes of major rivers.

the most savage persecution. In 303 CE, he began executing thousands of Christians for refusing to give up their faith. He also ordered the burning of all Christian texts and the destruction of the homes of Christians.

UNDERGROUND MEETINGS

In the city of Rome, Christians often held secret meetings in the catacombs. These were a series of tunnels under the city that were used as burial places. Christian paintings and altars dating from the fourth century have been found in the Roman catacombs.

The remains of a catacomb beneath the city of Rome, known as the Catacomb of Priscilla. Some of the catacombs where early Christians met had paintings of Jesus on their walls.

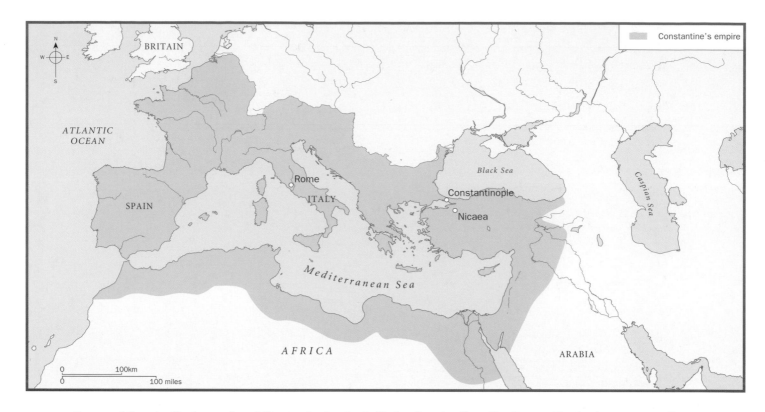

A map of Constantine's empire at its greatest extent. Under Constantine, the Roman Empire became a safe place for Christians to live.

Bishops, deacons and priests

In spite of the persecutions, Christianity continued to grow. By the start of the second century CE, the Christian communities had begun to organize themselves. Groups of Christians built churches where they met regularly for simple services. Each major city had its own bishop, who was responsible for all the Christians in the surrounding area. The bishops were helped by deacons and priests. The deacons took care of practical matters, such as giving help to the poor, while the priests travelled from church to church, leading services.

To keep the Christian Church united, the bishops communicated with each other as much as possible. In the third century, the leading bishops were based in Rome, Alexandria (Egypt) and Antioch (Turkey).

Constantine and the Christians

Emperor Diocletian died in 305, and the following year a new and ambitious ruler called Constantine came to power. At this stage in its history, the Roman Empire was divided in two: Constantine shared control of the Western Empire with Maxentius, while two more rulers controlled the Eastern Empire.

In 312, Constantine fought Maxentius at the Battle of Milvian Bridge, close to Rome. Just before the battle, Constantine had a vision. He saw a cross of light in the sky and heard a voice saying 'Conquer by this sign'. Constantine immediately gave orders for all his soldiers to paint the Christian Chi-Rho symbol on their shields (see panel on page 17). His army was victorious, and Constantine became convinced that he should support the Christians in his empire.

The Edict of Milan

After his victory over Maxentius, Constantine announced that Christians throughout the Western Empire were free to follow their religion. This famous announcement, made in 313, was known as the Edict of Milan. Constantine also gave money to the bishops to build large churches, known as basilicas, including the splendid basilica of St Peter's in Rome. Constantine announced that Sunday should be a day of rest, and he paid for new copies of the scriptures to be made.

In 324, Constantine defeated the rulers of the Eastern Empire and took control of the whole Roman Empire. Three years later, he moved his capital from Rome to the city of Byzantium (present-day Istanbul), which he renamed Constantinople. Constantine established Constantinople as a Christian city, with many fine churches.

The Council of Nicaea

During Constantine's rule, a violent argument broke out between two Christian thinkers. Arius, an Egyptian priest, claimed that Jesus Christ was created by God the Father, but Athanasius, the bishop of Alexandria, said that Christ was part of God and had existed from the beginning of time. This argument threatened to split the Church, so Constantine took action. He summoned all the bishops in the empire to a meeting at Nicaea (in present-day Turkey). At the Council of Nicaea in 325, the bishops decided to support Athanasius. They created a statement of their beliefs, which later became known as the Nicene Creed. This creed is still spoken by Christians today. It states that God the Son is 'of one substance with the Father'.

CHRISTIAN SIGNS

The early Christians used secret signs to show that they shared the same faith. These symbols included a fish, an anchor and a dove. The symbol that Constantine chose to paint on his soldiers' shields was the Chi-Rho sign. It is made up of the first two letters of the word *Christ* in Greek.

This Roman coin shows the Emperor Constantine wearing a crown of olive leaves. It was made in France around the year 306.

SAINT AUGUSTINE OF HIPPO

St Augustine was bishop of Hippo in North Africa from 396 to 430. He was a great thinker, who wrote many books on the Christian faith. In particular, Augustine explained that sinners may be forgiven through God's grace. Augustine's ideas had a great effect on Christian teaching. He is known as one of the Fathers of the Church. Augustine witnessed the collapse of the Roman Empire and wrote a famous book called *The City of God*. In it he stressed the importance of a united Christian community, which was separate from the state.

A detail from an Italian painting of Saint Augustine.

A state religion About 25 years after Constantine's death, the emperor Julian tried to bring back the Roman gods and goddesses, but it was too late to stop the growth of Christianity. All the emperors after Julian supported the Christians, and in 391 CE the emperor Theodosius declared that Christianity was the empire's official religion. By this time, the Christian Church had become wealthy and powerful. Christians built grand churches and held elaborate services, with chants and singing.

Rome takes control During the fourth century, the bishops held several councils to establish the form of services and to fix the times of the great festivals of the Christian year. At these councils, the bishop of Rome played a leading role. Gradually, the bishop of Rome became the head of the Church, and gained the new title of pope.

Hermits, monks and nuns Some Christians chose to spend their lives as hermits, living alone in caves in the desert. One famous hermit, St Simon Stylites, spent 30 years sitting on top of a pillar! But not everyone wanted to live as a hermit. In the fourth century, groups of men and women began to form single-sex communities, separated from the rest of society. Male communities were called monasteries, and men living there were called monks. Female communities were called convents, and the women were known as nuns.

The fall of the Roman Empire By the 350s, the Roman Empire was under threat from barbarian tribes. These were large groups of fierce warriors, most of them pagans who worshipped their own gods. In 401, an army of Visigoths attacked the city of Milan in northern Italy, and in 410 they invaded Rome. The Romans fought back, but meanwhile hordes of Vandals and other tribes poured into Germany and France. In 409, the Vandals invaded Spain, and 20 years later they conquered North Africa. From here, the Vandals moved into Italy, and in 455 they spent 12 days looting Rome. The Roman Empire in the west finally collapsed in 476. This was a major blow for Christianity.

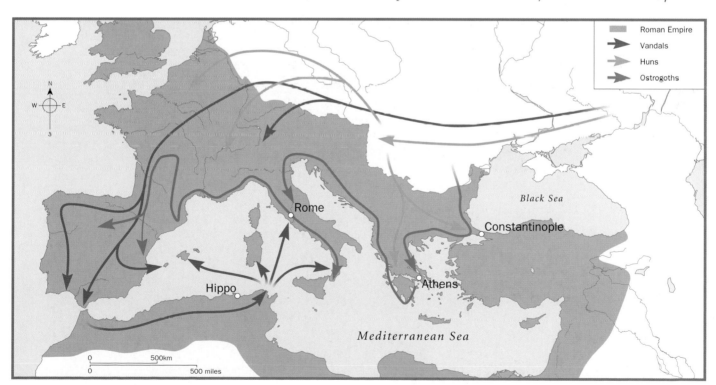

A map of the Roman Empire showing the routes taken by barbarian invaders. The empire in the west collapsed in 476, but the Eastern Empire, with its capital in Constantinople, managed to resist the invasions and survived for another thousand years.

CHAPTER 4:
THE CHURCH IN THE MIDDLE AGES

After the fall of Rome in 476, the Western Empire split into small barbarian kingdoms. In many parts of Europe, Christianity died out completely, but the Church survived in Rome. Some monasteries also survived, and monks kept Christian learning alive by copying out holy texts.

Spreading the message Gradually, Christian monks in the west began to spread their faith through Europe. One of the first areas to be converted to Christianity was Ireland. In the first half of the fifth century, St Patrick set up Christian monasteries in many parts of Ireland. These monasteries provided a base for other missionaries, who took the Christian message to Britain and France.

In 596, Pope Gregory the Great sent a monk called Augustine to preach to the Angles in southern England.

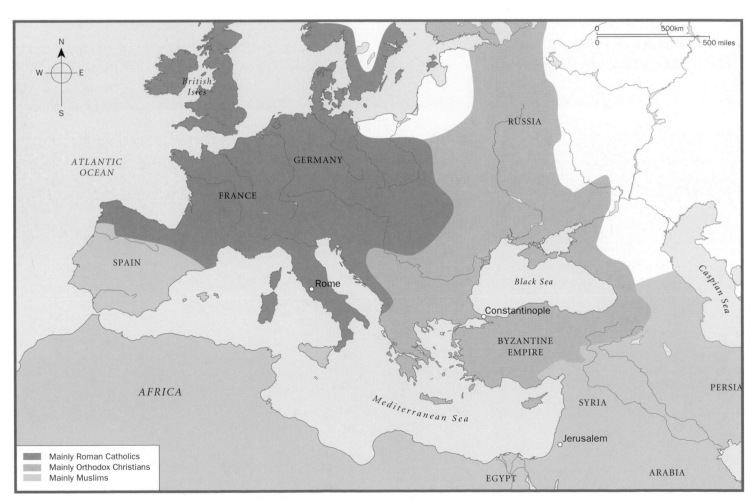

Mainly Roman Catholics
Mainly Orthodox Christians
Mainly Muslims

A map showing the Churches of the east and west after the split in 1054. The map also shows the extent of Islam (the religion of the Muslims) at this time.

Two centuries later, the English monk St Boniface converted the tribes of present-day Germany. The Viking people of Scandinavia took longer to accept Christianity, but by the 11th century there were churches in Denmark, Sweden and Norway.

The eastern Church While the Church in the west was slowly rebuilding itself, the Church in the eastern part of the Roman Empire was thriving. The capital of the Eastern, or Byzantine, Empire was Constantinople, and this became a very important centre for Christianity. Missionaries from the eastern Church carried their religion eastwards. In the ninth century, St Cyril and St Methodius took the Christian message to the Slavs in eastern Europe, and in 988 Prince Vladimir of Russia declared that all Russians should be baptized as Christians.

The Middle East

Christianity spread through Syria and Persia, but many Christians in these areas rebelled against the standard teachings of the Church. In Syria the rebels were known as Monophysites, and in Persia they were called Nestorians. Neither of these groups was recognized by the leaders of the Church.

In the seventh century, the new religion of Islam began in Arabia. Within a hundred years, Islam had spread widely, reaching large areas of the Middle East, as well as North Africa and southern Spain. A few Christian communities survived in these areas, but Christians were greatly outnumbered by Muslims (followers of Islam).

The East–West split

Gradually, the Church in the east became increasingly independent from the western Church, and, after many quarrels, the Churches decided to split in 1054. The eastern Church was led by the patriarch in Constantinople, while the western Church was led by the pope in Rome. Later, the eastern Church became known as the Orthodox Church, and the western Church came to be called the Roman Catholic Church.

CHRISTIANITY IN ETHIOPIA

In the fourth century, a Christian missionary named Frumentius was shipwrecked off the coast of Ethiopia, in North Africa. He converted the king of the ancient Ethiopian kingdom of Axum. Two centuries later, the area that is now Sudan also became Christian. Even after North Africa was taken over by Muslim rulers, Ethiopia remained a largely Christian kingdom (see map on page 37).

The city of Constantinople (later called Istanbul) was the heart of the eastern Church and was full of splendid church buildings. This photograph shows the dome of the Church of Hagia Sophia in Istanbul.

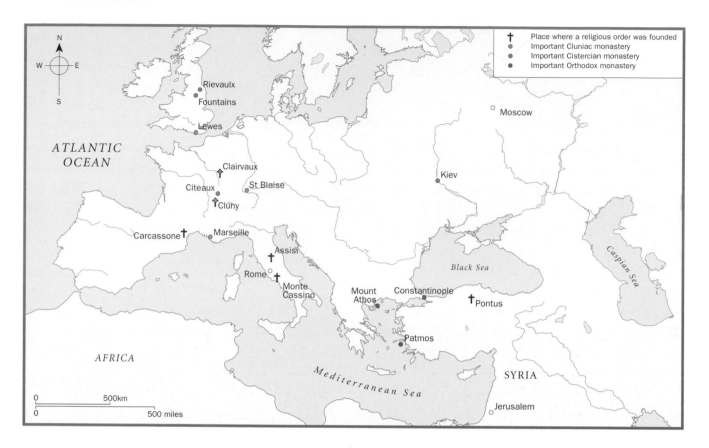

This map shows some of the most important Christian monasteries in the Middle Ages. It also shows the places where religious orders were founded.

The growth of the monasteries

During the fourth and fifth centuries, the monasteries became more organized. This was especially due to two men – St Basil in the east (see panel on page 23) and St Benedict in the west.

Saint Benedict's rule

St Benedict was born in northern Italy in 480. He began his religious life as a hermit, but he soon decided it was best for monks to live together in a community. He established a famous monastery at Monte Cassino and wrote a set of guidelines for his monks to follow.

According to St Benedict's rule, monks should divide their time between prayer, study and hard physical work, such as farming. He taught his followers to meet together to worship at regular times of day. He also stated that monks should eat plain food, wear simple clothes (called habits) and look after the sick and the poor. After Benedict's death, Benedictine monasteries were set up all over western Europe.

Cluniacs and Cistercians

In the tenth century, Abbot Odilo became the new head of the Benedictine monastery of Cluny in central France. He established a new kind of monastery that concentrated on learning, music and art. Cluniac monasteries soon spread all over France. Their buildings were beautifully decorated, and the Cluniac monks held elaborate services. However, another French abbot, St Bernard of Clairvaux, reacted against the richness of the Cluniac monasteries. He set up a new order of monks known as the Cistercians, who led a simple life of prayer in much plainer buildings. The Cistercian movement was very popular in the 12th and 13th centuries.

Franciscans and Dominicans

In the early 13th century, some new religious orders (or groups) was founded. These were orders of friars, who lived simple lives, like monks, but who spent most of their time travelling around, preaching and caring for the poor and sick.

Two men were responsible for the growth of the friars: St Dominic and St Francis. Dominic was a Spanish missionary who worked for the Church, trying to convert heretics (people who held beliefs that contradicted the Church's teachings). In 1215, Dominic founded an order of preachers to specialize in teaching. The order was later known as the Dominicans. The first Dominican community was based near Carcassonne in southern France. Later in his life, Dominic also created an order of Dominican nuns.

St Francis came from the Italian town of Assisi. He led a holy life, teaching and caring for the poor. Francis soon attracted many followers, and in 1209 he established the order of Franciscan friars in Assisi. Three years later, St Clare, a friend of St Francis, set up the order of the Poor Clares for women. Like the Franciscans, the Poor Clares lived in simple buildings and spent most of their time helping the poor.

ORTHODOX MONASTERIES

In the mid-fourth century, St Basil the Great founded a monastery in Pontus (south of the Black Sea). He wrote a set of rules for his monks, instructing them to pray, to carry out good works, to help the sick and the poor, and to study the Bible. Over the next few centuries, many more monasteries were founded in Turkey and Greece, all of them following St Basil's rule.

A medieval painting showing St Benedict giving his blessing to the members of his order.

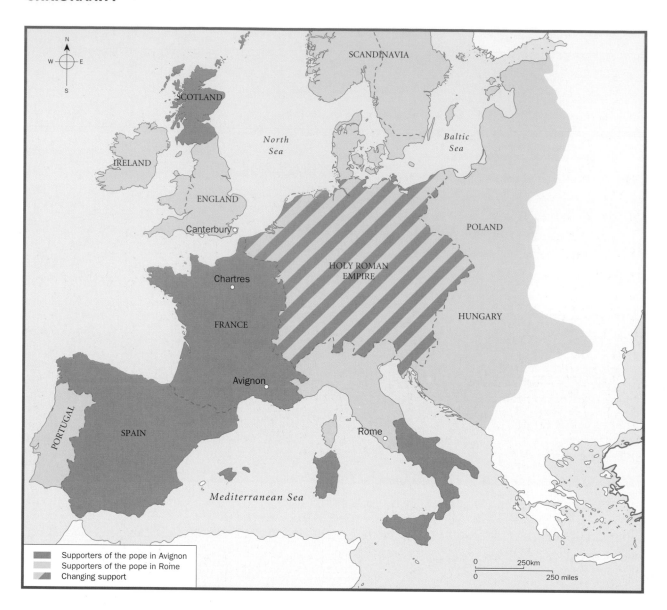

A map of medieval Europe, showing the followers of the rival popes, based in Avignon and Rome. The Holy Roman emperors kept changing sides, sometimes supporting one pope, sometimes the other.

Church and state

The pope was the head of the western Church, but he also had to rely on the help of secular (non-religious) rulers, such as kings and emperors. During the Middle Ages, there were times when the popes and rulers supported each other. However, there were often dramatic power struggles.

Charlemagne's empire

One of the Church's great early supporters was the emperor Charlemagne. He became leader of the Franks in 768 and built up a large Christian empire, which covered most of present-day Germany and France. In 800, Pope Leo III crowned Charlemagne emperor of the Romans, and Charlemagne promised to support the Church. This alliance with Charlemagne gave the Church a great deal of power. However, after Charlemagne's death, his empire collapsed.

The Holy Roman Empire

In 955, the German leader Otto I won control of large parts of central and eastern Europe. The pope granted Otto and his descendants the title of Holy Roman Emperor. This title gave the emperors control over all the bishops in their lands, and they used the bishops to help them rule. However, the popes wanted to control the bishops themselves, and they hoped to gain money from the bishops' lands. During the Middle Ages, the popes and emperors had many fierce quarrels over their rights to control the bishops and their lands.

Popes in France

In 1309, two men competed for the title of pope. One of them appealed to the French king for help and moved to Avignon in southern France, while the rival pope stayed in Rome. For the next hundred years, the official popes were based in France and, for part of this time, rival popes ruled in Rome.

Some countries in western Europe followed the Avignon pope, while others supported the pope in

Rome (see map on page 24). The situation was made even more complicated because the Holy Roman emperors kept changing sides. This major split in the Church was called the Great Schism of the West. It greatly weakened the power of the Roman Catholic popes and bishops.

PILGRIMAGES

During the Middle Ages, many Christians went on pilgrimages. They travelled long distances to holy shrines, where saints were buried or sacred objects were kept. Pilgrims made these journeys in the hope that God would forgive their sins and cure their diseases.

Many people made a pilgrimage to Jerusalem or Rome. In England, pilgrims visited the shrine of St Thomas Becket in Canterbury. Becket was an archbishop who quarrelled with King Henry II and was murdered in 1170 by the king's knights.

This painting of English pilgrims comes from an illustrated version of the *Canterbury Tales* by Geoffrey Chaucer. The *Canterbury Tales*, written in the 14th century, introduces a group of pilgrims who make a pilgrimage from London to Canterbury and tell stories along the way.

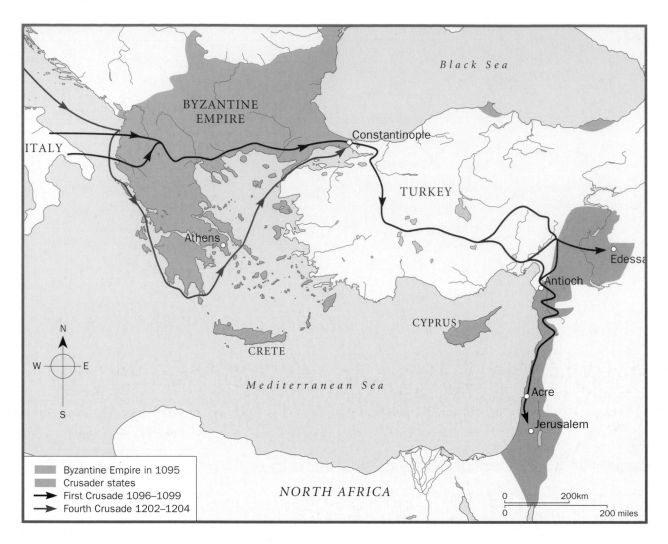

A map showing the routes taken by different Crusades and the land won by the Crusaders.

Muslims and Christians

By the end of the 11th century, many Christians were worried about the Holy Land. For 400 years, Palestine had been ruled by Muslim Turks, and for most of that time the Turks had allowed Christian pilgrims to travel to Jerusalem. However, by the 1090s, relations between Turks and Christians had become much worse, and some pilgrims had been attacked.

Christians in the eastern Church felt especially threatened by the Turks. The Turkish lands lay next to the Christian Byzantine Empire, and the Turks were gradually winning more and more Byzantine lands. This alarmed Christians in both the eastern and western Churches.

The Crusades begin

In 1095, Pope Urban II preached a sermon, urging all Christians to go on a 'holy war', or Crusade, to drive the Muslims out of the Holy Land. Nobles from France, Germany and Italy gathered their armies together and set off on the long journey to the Middle East. This was the start of the First Crusade.

In 1099, the Crusaders captured Jerusalem and the surrounding lands. Some Crusaders stayed on to defend their newly conquered territory, but many others returned home. In 1144, a Muslim army seized the city of Edessa (in present-day Turkey), and the Second Crusade failed to win it back. In 1187, the Muslims, led by Saladin, recaptured Jerusalem.

Later Crusades

The Third Crusade was led by the rulers of France, England and Germany. They won many battles and captured the city of Acre, but they did not succeed in winning back Jerusalem.

CRUSADER KNIGHTS

During the Crusades, some new orders of warrior monks were formed, known as Crusader knights. These men lived like monks, dedicating their lives to God, but they were also fierce warriors. The main orders of Crusader knights were the Knights Templar, the Knights Hospitaller and the Teutonic Knights.

A medieval artist's impression of the capture of the city of Antioch. The Crusaders won Antioch from the Muslim Turks during the First Crusade.

The Fourth Crusade only reached as far as Constantinople. Here, the Crusaders turned on the Byzantines and took over their city. Crusaders from western Europe ruled Constantinople for the next 60 years and sent many Byzantine treasures back home. This shameful period created deep divisions between the eastern and western Churches.

Over the next 100 years there were three more Crusades, but the Christians did not win any major new lands. In 1229, the Muslims agreed that the Christians could take back Jerusalem. However, this agreement did not last. In 1244, a Muslim army recaptured Jerusalem, and, in 1291, the Muslims finally conquered Acre, the last Crusader city. This marked the end of the Crusades.

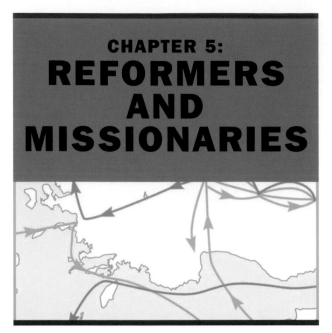

CHAPTER 5:
REFORMERS AND MISSIONARIES

In the early years of the 16th century, some determined individuals began to make public protests about the Roman Catholic Church. At first these protesters simply aimed to reform the Church, but instead their protests led to the creation of some entirely new Christian groups. The dramatic reshaping of the western Church in the 16th century is known as the Reformation, and the members of the new Churches became known as Protestants or Nonconformists.

Problems in the Church By the early 1500s, many people in western Europe were unhappy with the Roman Catholic Church. Too many Church leaders seemed to be interested only in wealth and power, and people complained that their parish priests were badly educated and lazy. In particular, people blamed the Church for the sale of indulgences (pardons for people's sins). Rich people paid large sums of money for these indulgences, while the poor could not afford to have their sins pardoned.

Martin Luther In 1517, a German priest called Martin Luther wrote a list of 95 ways in which the Catholic Church could be reformed. He nailed this list to the church door in Wittenberg (in northern Germany), and his ideas soon spread. This made the leaders of the Church very angry, and in 1520 the pope excommunicated Luther (banned him from the Church forever).

Luther went into hiding and worked on his ideas of how the Church should be run. He believed that church services should be kept simple and that people should read the Bible for themselves rather than having it read to them by a priest. Luther helped to make this possible by translating the New Testament from Greek into German.

One of the earliest copies of Luther's Bible, translated from Greek into German. This copy was owned by Luther himself and inlcudes notes and corrections made by him.

A PLAINER STYLE

Protestant churches are generally much plainer in style than Roman Catholic churches. Unlike Catholic churches, they do not have any statues of the Virgin Mary or the saints because Protestants believe that they should communicate directly with God and Jesus rather than praying to Mary and the saints. The one exception to this practice is the Anglican Church. This is a Protestant Church, but it took over the buildings of the Roman Catholics (see pages 30–31). Many Anglican churches have statues of saints.

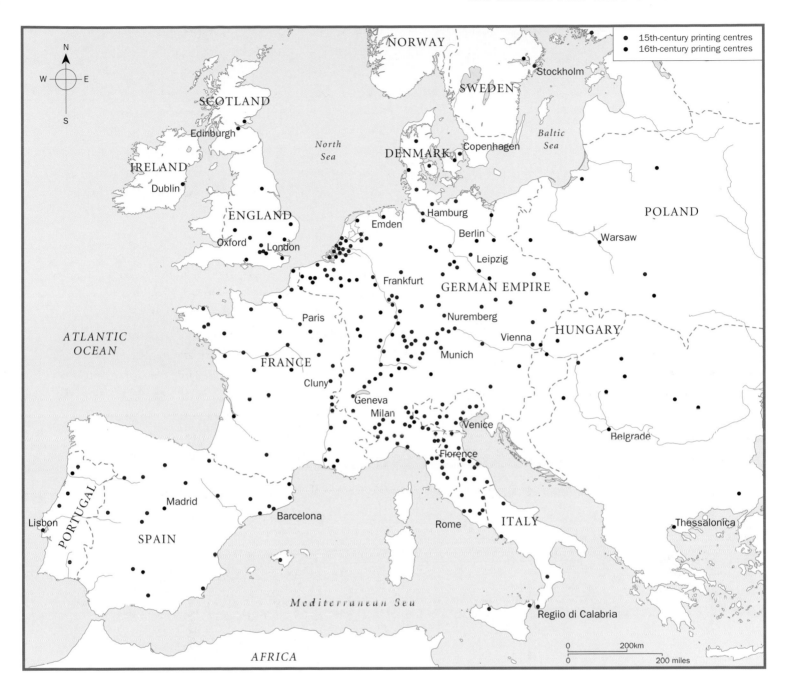

A map of Europe showing the location of the major printing presses in the 15th and 16th centuries.

Luther had intended to reform the Catholic Church from the inside, but by the 1520s it was clear that this was impossible. Gradually people all over Germany began to hold simple services, based on Luther's ideas, and the Lutheran Church was born. By the 1550s, Lutheranism had spread to Denmark, Norway and Sweden. Other Protestant churches followed the example of the Lutherans and held simple services with readings from the Bible and singing of hymns.

The printing press The development of printing played a key role in the rapid spread of Luther's ideas. In 1436, the German Johannes Gutenberg had invented the printing press and by 1500 there were presses all over Europe, but especially in Germany (see map). Luther was a gifted and popular writer who wrote many pamphlets, which were printed and circulated widely. Thanks to the printing press, ordinary people could also read Luther's translation of the Bible.

Calvinism

John Calvin was a French priest who broke away from the Roman Catholic Church. In 1541, he established a group of Protestants in Geneva, Switzerland. Like Luther, Calvin emphasized the importance of the Bible in Christian worship. He also claimed that some chosen people would be saved and go to heaven, while others would go to hell. Calvin wrote several books on the Bible, which were widely read in Europe. Calvinism was very popular in Switzerland, and it also spread to Scotland and the Netherlands.

Henry VIII's rebellion

The English Protestant revolt began when King Henry VIII quarrelled with the pope. Henry wanted to divorce his first wife, Catherine of Aragon, and marry his mistress, Anne Boleyn. But the pope refused to grant him a divorce. This made Henry so angry that he decided to break away from the Catholic Church. In an act of Parliament of 1534, Henry was named supreme head of the Church of England. This was the start of the Anglican Church.

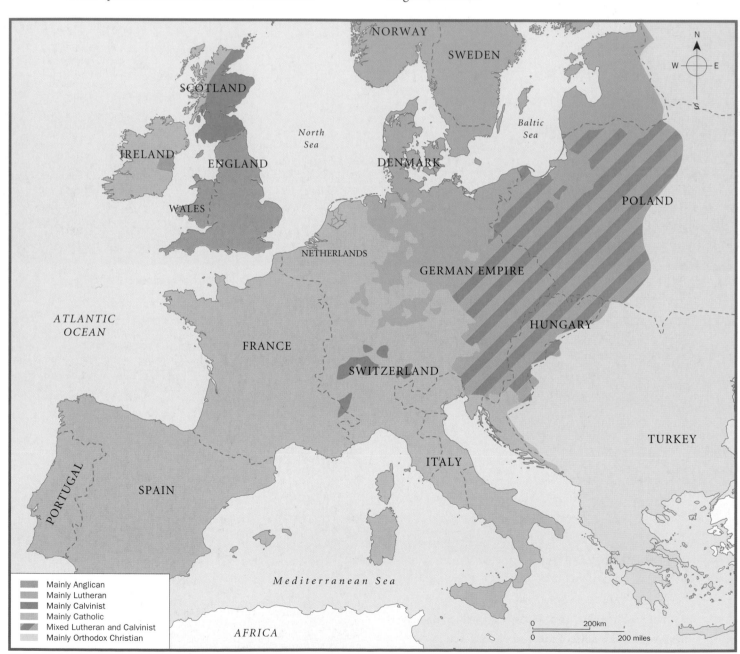

Key:
- Mainly Anglican
- Mainly Lutheran
- Mainly Calvinist
- Mainly Catholic
- Mixed Lutheran and Calvinist
- Mainly Orthodox Christian

A map of religious groups in Europe at the end of the Reformation, around 1560.

The dissolution of the monasteries, by King Henry VIII, led to many fine buildings failing into ruins. One of the many ruined monasteries is Rievaulx Abbey in Yorkshire, England.

In some ways the Anglican Church simply continued the practices of the Roman Catholic Church. It still had bishops and parish priests and it took over all the Catholic cathedrals and churches. However, there were some differences. Bibles were placed in Anglican churches for the public to read, and services were held in English, not in Latin. In 1549, the Archbishop of Canterbury, Thomas Cranmer, produced the *Book of Common Prayer*, which outlined all the services of the Anglican Church. Today, Anglicans around the world use prayer books based on Cranmer's original work.

In 1538, Henry VIII began a campaign of dissolving (or closing down) the Catholic monasteries in his kingdom. It was well known that many monks and nuns did not lead holy lives, but Henry also wanted to destroy the power and wealth of the Catholic Church in England. Some of the monastery buildings were sold to wealthy nobles, but many others simply fell into ruins.

THE PRESBYTERIAN CHURCH

The Presbyterian Church began in Scotland in the 1560s. It was founded by John Knox, who had spent several years as a preacher at a Calvinist church in Geneva (Switzerland). In the Presbyterian Church there is no fixed form of worship, and each congregation is governed by a group of presbyters, or elders, who are all of equal rank.

When James I became king of England in 1603, he recognized Presbyterianism as the national faith in Scotland. Presbyterianism later spread to England, Wales, Ireland and North America.

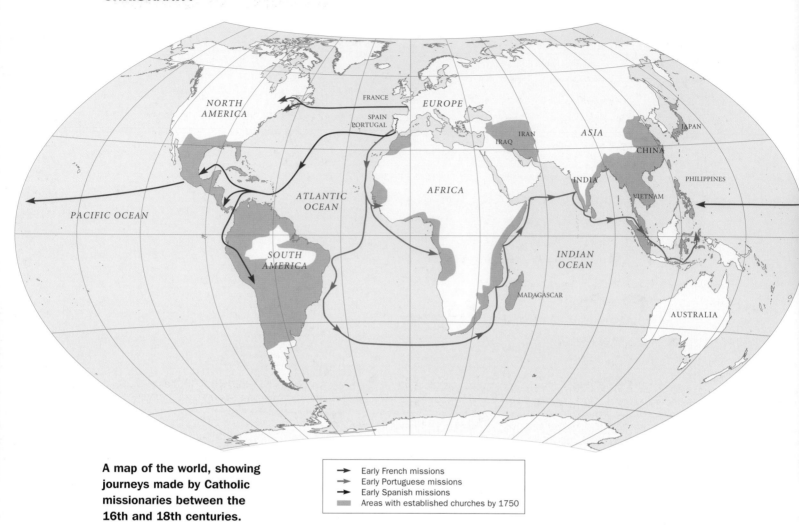

A map of the world, showing journeys made by Catholic missionaries between the 16th and 18th centuries.

→ Early French missions
→ Early Portuguese missions
→ Early Spanish missions
▓ Areas with established churches by 1750

The Counter-Reformation As the
Reformation gathered strength, the Roman Catholic leaders tried hard to win people back to their Church. They began a reform movement of their own, which became known as the Counter-Reformation.

Some of the first areas of reform concerned the monasteries. The existing monastic orders were reformed and several new orders were created. Catholic leaders set up training colleges for priests, built elaborate new cathedrals and churches, and attacked the Protestants in sermons and books. From 1545 to 1563, the leaders of the Church met together in a group known as the Council of Trent. They used the council to restate their beliefs, condemn Protestant ideas, and plan reforms to the Church.

The Jesuits The most famous of the new
monastic orders was the Society of Jesus, also known as the Jesuits. The Jesuits were founded in 1534 by the Spanish monk Ignatius Loyola. They lived a life of extreme discipline and devotion to Christ and also promised to carry out any task the pope demanded of them. The Jesuits ran schools and colleges and travelled as missionaries, first to Poland and then on to more distant lands.

Catholic missionaries From the early
1500s onwards, Catholic missionaries began to accompany conquering armies to newly discovered lands in South America, Africa and Asia (see map). Jesuit missionaries were especially adventurous. Francis Xavier, for example, led missions to India, Sri Lanka and Japan in the 1540s and 1550s, while Matteo Ricci travelled to China in 1582 and stayed there for the next 20 years.

By the start of the 17th century, Catholic missionaries had converted hundreds of thousands of people to Christianity and set up churches, monasteries and schools in many parts of Asia and South America. However, not all the missions were successful. In the 1640s, a group of French Jesuit missionaries in Canada were put to death by Native Americans.

Religious wars In many parts of Europe, the clash between Protestants and Catholics led to war. In Germany, Lutherans and Catholics fought each other in the Thirty Years' War (1618–1648), while in France, French Protestants, known as Huguenots, fought the Catholic king and his supporters. The most horrific event during the wars fought in France was the St Bartholomew's Day massacre of 1572, when thousands of Huguenots were killed on a single day.

BAROQUE ART

During the time of the Counter Reformation, a new style of religious art and architecture developed. Known as Baroque, it was very elaborate and was popular with many Church leaders because it played on people's emotions and encouraged them to be more devout. Baroque painters and sculptors, such as Gianlorenzo Bernini, produced dramatic images of saints experiencing miraculous visions, and martyrs suffering terrible deaths.

The Ecstasy of Saint Teresa was created by Gianlorenzo Bernini between 1647 and 1652. Works like this had a powerful emotional effect on Catholic Christians.

QUAKERS

The Society of Friends – or the Quakers – was founded in England around 1650. Quakers gather in meeting houses rather than churches and they stress the importance of quiet meditation. Soon after the Society of Friends was formed, some Quakers travelled to North America, but they faced persecution there from the larger Christian groups. In the 1670s, a Quaker called William Penn began to buy up land for the Quakers in the area that would later become Pennsylvania, USA. Today, a number of Quaker organizations have their headquarters in Pennsylvania.

Puritans The Puritan movement developed in England in the 16th century, when some Protestants became unhappy with the Anglican Church under Queen Elizabeth I (1558–1603). The Puritans disapproved of all finery and show. They dressed very plainly and followed a simple form of worship.

By the 1650s, the Puritans had gained political power in England. In the previous decade there had been a power struggle between the English king, Charles I, and Parliament (the law-making assembly), and this struggle

① Massachusetts
② New Hampshire
③ New York
④ Rhode Island
⑤ Connecticut
⑥ Pennsylvania
⑦ New Jersey
⑧ Delaware
⑨ Maryland
⑩ Virginia
⑪ North Carolina
⑫ South Carolina
⑬ Georgia

Lutherans
Congregationalists
Presbyterians
Baptists

A map of the North American colonies in 1750, showing the main Christian groups. The Lutheran and Congregationalist Churches both had a strong following, but no single religious group dominated the colonies.

led to a civil war (1642–1649). Parliament's forces were triumphant, and one of their leaders, Oliver Cromwell, took power. Cromwell was a Puritan and, from 1653 to 1658, he ruled England according to Puritan principles. He closed down many ale houses and discouraged dancing and theatre-going. However, in 1660, Charles I's son, Charles II, became king and made Anglicanism the official religion of England.

Baptists Like the Puritans, the Baptists were a breakaway group from the Anglican Church. Originally known as Separatists, they were persecuted in England and escaped to Holland in 1608. The Separatists returned to England in 1612 and attracted many followers. By the following century, the Baptist Church was well-established in Europe and America. Baptists only baptize adult believers, because Christ was not baptized until he was an adult. In the Baptist Church, baptism is performed by total immersion in water.

Christians in North America In 1620, a group of Puritans and Separatists known as the Pilgrims set sail from England to North America. They arrived in Plymouth, Massachusetts, on the east coast and established a colony there. Over the next century, Protestants from England, Scotland, Germany and the Netherlands all made the journey to North America. Most of them settled in the east and north of the continent, and these areas became strongly Protestant.

In other parts of North America, away from the east and north, the Catholic religion was dominant. The French owned large amounts of land in the centre of the continent, until this was sold to the USA in the 19th century. From the 1500s onwards, The Spanish had settled in the western part of America. In both the central and western areas, Roman Catholicism was the main religion of the settlers.

The First Great Awakening In the 1730s, a young church minister called Jonathan Edwards began to travel around the east coast of the USA preaching with great passion. Edwards' sermons had a dramatic effect on his listeners and won thousands of converts to Christianity. Edwards' followers built new churches all over New England, and he inspired many other preachers to spread the word. This dramatic movement later became known as the First Great Awakening.

Once the Pilgrims had become settled in Plymouth, they held a service of thanksgiving to God. This painting shows the first sermon delivered in Plymouth.

CHAPTER 6:
INTO THE MODERN WORLD

In the 18th century, some Christian preachers began to travel from place to place, spreading their message of salvation. They held open-air meetings in which they preached and encouraged people to pray and sing hymns together. This type of worship, in which the Christian message is taken into the wider world, is often known as evangelism. One of the first evangelist Christians was John Wesley, who developed Methodism.

John Wesley and the Methodists

John Wesley trained as an Anglican minister, but in 1738 he experienced a dramatic conversion and began to spread the message that Christians could be saved from their sins. At first, he preached his message in Anglican churches, but later he travelled around the country holding open-air meetings wherever he went.

Methodists hold simple services, which involve the singing of rousing hymns and the preaching of

THE SALVATION ARMY

In 1861, William Booth, a Methodist minister, and his wife Catherine, began a Christian mission to help the poor in the East End of London. To carry out this work, he set up an organization called the Salvation Army. Booth's army of men and women dressed in easily recognizable uniforms and held lively services in the street, attracting large crowds with their cheerful band music. As well as teaching the gospel, the Salvation Army offered shelter and food to people in need. By 1912, the army had branches in more than 50 countries.

Evangeline Booth, daughter of William and Catherine Booth, was for many years one of the leaders of the Salvation Army. Here she is shown raising money for the Salvation Army's work.

passionate sermons. They also aim to live a virtuous life and help the poor. John Wesley made sure that the Methodist Church was very well organized, and used travelling preachers to spread the word. His movement grew rapidly in Britain and the USA.

The Second Great Awakening

Around the end of the 18th century, a powerful new wave of religious feeling swept through the USA. Known as the Second Great Awakening, it started with 'camp meetings' held in tents in Kentucky and Tennessee. People stayed for days in the camps, listening to fiery sermons and being baptized in their thousands in the local rivers. Later, this Christian revival spread to the East Coast, where powerful preachers such as Lyman Beecher and Charles Finney drew enormous crowds.

Many of the newly converted Christians worked to change American society. In particular, the Second Great Awakening led many people to campaign against the practice of keeping slaves.

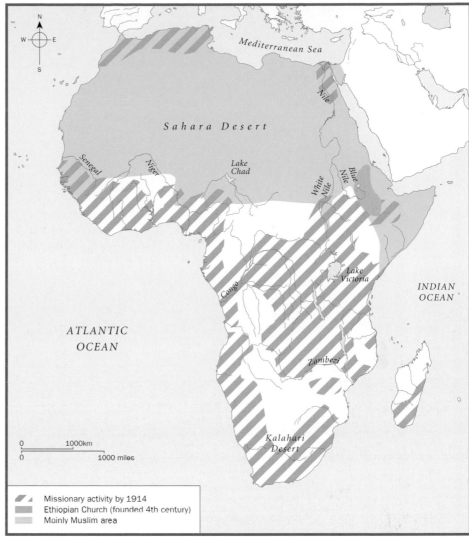

A map of Africa in 1914, showing all the areas reached by Christian missionaries. The map also shows the ancient Christian community of Ethiopia.

Legend:
- Missionary activity by 1914
- Ethiopian Church (founded 4th century)
- Mainly Muslim area

New religious groups

During the 19th century, several new sects (or branches) of Christianity were founded in the USA. These new religious groups were usually founded by someone who preached a new 'revelation' of the Bible's message. Some of the most successful sects were the Mormons, the Christian Scientists and the Jehovah's Witnesses. These three religious groups soon gained large numbers of followers around the world.

Christian missionaries

By the 1850s, countries such as Britain, Germany and France had built up large colonies in Africa and Asia. Christians were

determined to spread their faith to these areas, and missionaries from Europe travelled to all parts of their empires and beyond. By 1900, Christian missionaries had managed to establish churches in almost every country of the world.

Many Christian missionaries did more than build churches and teach Christianity. They also set up hospitals and schools and helped to introduce new farming methods. A major part of missionary work was providing people with copies of the Bible in their own language, so they could read it for themselves. By 1900, the New Testament had been translated into over 500 languages.

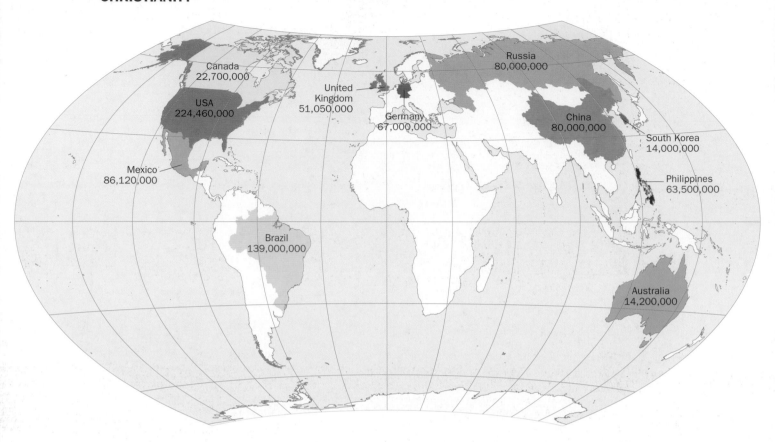

Canada
22,700,000

Russia
80,000,000

United
Kingdom
51,050,000

USA
224,460,000

Germany
67,000,000

China
80,000,000

South Korea
14,000,000

Mexico
86,120,000

Philippines
63,500,000

Brazil
139,000,000

Australia
14,200,000

The Charismatic movement Around the start of the 20th century, a new Christian movement, known as the Pentecostal Church, began in Los Angeles, USA. Pentecostal Christians are now often known as Charismatic Christians, or simply Charismatics. They hold very lively services in which everyone takes part in a wholehearted way, and some of their members claim to have the gifts of prophecy and healing.

By the 1950s, the Charismatic movement had spread throughout the world. In 2000, the movement had an estimated 500 million members, making it the fastest-growing movement within the Christian Church worldwide. Today, it is especially popular in South America.

A map of the world in about 2000, showing just a few of the countries with a significant proportion of Christians. The map gives approximate numbers for Christians in those countries.

THE ORTHODOX CHURCH

After the Orthodox Church split from the Roman Catholic Church in 1054, it followed a very different path from the Church in the West. In 1453, Constantinople was conquered by Muslim Turks, and the Church in Turkey and the Middle East struggled to survive. However, In Greece and Russia, the Orthodox Church continued to thrive, although the Russians and Greeks developed different traditions.

In 1922, Russia formed a Communist state called the Soviet Union. The Soviet leaders saw Christianity as a major threat to their system of government. Within a few years more than a thousand bishops and priests had been executed, and hundreds of monasteries had been destroyed. Persecution of Christians continued until the collapse of the Soviet Union in 1991. Since then, the Church in Russia has experienced a dramatic revival.

The American evangelist Billy Graham has converted millions of people to Christianity. He is shown here preaching in New York.

Modern evangelism

In the 1950s, there was a new surge in evangelism, as people spread the Christian message through exciting sermons and rousing hymns. Evangelism was especially popular in the USA, where it was greatly helped by the emergence of television as a mass medium.

The leading evangelist of the 20th century was the American preacher Billy Graham. He has travelled around the world many times, speaking to an estimated 210 million people in 185 countries.

Televangelists

Over the last 20 years, there have been a growing number of 'televangelists' who spread their message through television. As well as conducting televised services, some televangelists also provide commentary on current events. In the USA there are several TV channels entirely devoted to programmes with a strongly Christian message.

Liberation theology

In the 1970s, a new movement began within the Roman Catholic Church in South America. Known as liberation theology, it is based on the idea that Christians have a duty to help the poor and the suffering. Followers of liberation theology believe that they should defend their people against systems of government that keep a few people rich and powerful at the expense of the poor. Some priests in South America have made a stand against corrupt governments, and a few have been killed. For example, Archbishop Oscar Romero of El Salvador was murdered in 1980 for standing up for the rights of the poor in his country.

Christianity today

At the start of the 21st century, Christianity is the world's largest religion. Over a third of the world's population describe themselves as Christians. With more than two billion Christians worldwide, Christianity has almost twice as many followers as Islam, the world's second largest faith.

Different patterns

In Africa, much of Asia and parts of South America, Christianity is growing very fast. But in Europe the Christian religion is in decline. Attendance at church services in Europe fell dramatically in the second half of the 20th century, and now only 10 percent of Europeans are regular churchgoers. In the USA, however, Christianity is still very popular. The vast majority of Americans describe themselves as Christians, and up to 40 percent of the population attend church regularly.

Fundamentalists

The Christian Fundamentalist movement began in America in the early 20th century as a reaction to the growing lack of faith in modern society. Since then it has grown dramatically, although most of its followers are in the USA.

Fundamentalist Christians try to return to the basics (or fundamentals) of their religion, and emphasize the importance of complete belief in the Bible. They also campaign for strict moral standards in public and private life. Many Fundamentalists believe that God created the world in seven days. These 'creationists' reject the theory of evolution which states that humans are descended from apes.

Women priests

By the end of the 20th century, several Christian groups had decided to ordain women as priests or ministers. The Danish Lutherans led the way when they elected their first female priest in 1947. American Methodists and Presbyterians started ordaining women in 1956, and in 1988 the American Episcopalian Church (the American branch of the Anglican Church) elected its first woman bishop. In 1994, the Anglicans approved the ordination of women priests. However, there is still resistance to the idea of female priests in the Roman Catholic and Orthodox Churches.

Christianity is thriving in many parts of Asia. In 2004, around 100,000 South Koreans held a prayer meeting in a football stadium to celebrate Easter.

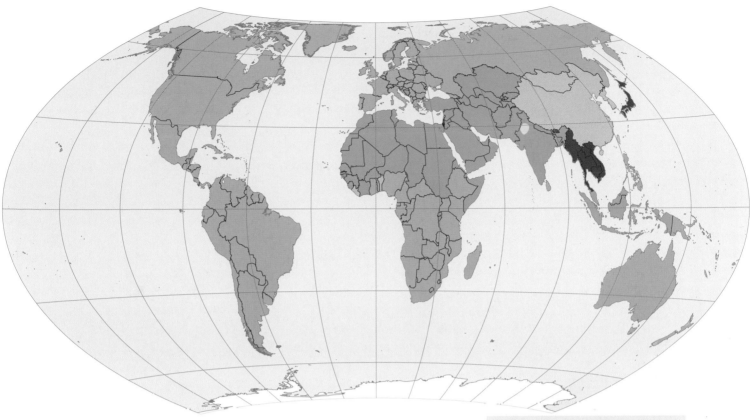

A map showing the location of the majority of Christians compared to people of other world faiths.

- Buddhism
- Christianity
- Hinduism
- Indigenous Religions
- Islam
- Judaism
- Non-religious
- Sikhism

Coming together

In recent years, the different denominations (or branches) of the Christian Church have made many efforts to understand each other and even work together. These efforts to encourage cooperation are known as the ecumenical movement. In 1948, the World Council of Churches was founded to encourage the ecumenical spirit. On a smaller scale, there are many shared activities between different denominations in local communities.

In 1964, Pope Paul VI visited Patriarch Athenagoras in Istanbul (formerly Constantinople). This was the first major attempt to heal the division between the Roman Catholic and Orthodox Churches since their split in 1054. Since this visit, there have been more meetings between popes and patriarchs.

One outstanding example of the ecumenical spirit is the Taizé community. This Christian community was founded by a Swiss monk, Brother Roger, in the French town of Taizé close to Lyons. The Taizé brothers hold simple services that can be shared by people of all denominations. Every year, thousands of people flock to Taizé to worship together.

GIVING AID

Some Christians see it as their duty to help the many people in the world who are suffering from poverty, hunger, and disease. Christian charities, such as Christian Aid, send money and support to people who are suffering, and many brave individuals devote their lives to helping others. In many parts of the world, Christians have set up hospitals and caring communities, which are often run by monks and nuns. The most famous of these nuns is Mother Teresa, who devoted her life to helping the poor and homeless in India (see page 43).

GREAT LIVES

Jesus (c. 4–c. 33 CE)

Jesus was born in Bethlehem in the Roman province of Judea and spent his childhood in Nazareth in northern Palestine. After his baptism by John the Baptist, Jesus began his adult work of preaching, performing miracles and healing the sick. He invited twelve disciples to help him in his work, and everywhere he went he gained more followers. Jesus spent most of his adult life in the area of Galilee in northern Palestine. In the final weeks of his life, he travelled to Jerusalem, where he was arrested, tried and sentenced to death by crucifixion. Christians believe that Jesus rose from the dead three days after his death.

St Paul (c. 3–c. 68)

Paul was originally named Saul. He was born in Tarsus (in present-day Turkey), the son of a Pharisee (a high-ranking Jewish priest). According to the Bible, Saul was converted to Christianity on the road to Damascus, and after his conversion he changed his name to Paul. He made a series of great missionary journeys through Syria, Turkey and Greece, and founded many Christian communities. Paul was eventually arrested in Jerusalem and sent to Rome for trial. In Rome, he was kept as a prisoner inside his house, but during this time he wrote many letters to the communities he had founded. These letters were later included in the New Testament. Nobody knows how Paul died, but he may have been put to death by the Roman emperor Nero.

St Benedict (c. 480–547)

St Benedict was the son of an Italian nobleman. He was educated in Rome, but while still a teenager he rejected the worldly life and went to live as a hermit. Gradually, Benedict's fame spread, and people came to join him. He built twelve monastic houses for his followers and encouraged them to live a simple life, dividing their time between hard physical work, study and prayer. After a few years, Benedict set up a second community in the mountain village of Monte Cassino. Benedict spent the rest of his life at Monte Cassino, and during this time wrote his famous rule, providing guidelines on how monks should live.

St Francis of Assisi (1182–1226)

St Francis was born in Assisi in northern Italy, the son of a rich merchant. At the age of about 24, he decided to give up all his possessions and live the life of a poor man, wandering the countryside and preaching the Christian message. He attracted many followers and created a community of 'brothers' who lived a simple life like him. Later, the brothers became known as friars. Francis was famous for the kindness and gentleness he showed to both people and animals. He went on several journeys, and everywhere he went he preached and cared for the poor.

Martin Luther (1483–1546)

Martin Luther was a brilliant scholar who also became a university teacher and a preacher. However, Luther grew increasingly unhappy about the corruption in the Catholic Church. In 1517, he wrote a list of Ninety-five Theses, outlining all the problems in the Catholic Church and posted them on the church door in Wittenberg. In 1520, the pope wrote a document condemning Luther's arguments, which Luther burnt in public. Luther was excommunicated and threatened with burning as a heretic. He went into hiding and worked on his ideas for a new kind of worship. Luther also translated the New Testament into German. He eventually returned to Wittenberg and spent the rest of his life preaching and spreading his ideas.

John Wesley (1703–1791)

John Wesley was born in Lincolnshire, England. He trained to be an Anglican minister at Oxford University. There, he joined a group of young men who were called 'the Methodists' because they lived according to very strict rules. In 1738, John Wesley experienced a 'conversion', in which he understood that Christ could save him. From then on, he devoted his life to preaching this message. John and his brother Charles preached in churches, on the streets and at public meetings. John Wesley organized his new Methodist church very well and encouraged the leaders of his Church to play an active part in social reforms.

FURTHER INFORMATION

Martin Luther King (1929–1968)

Martin Luther King was born in Atlanta, Georgia, USA. The son of a Baptist minister, King also trained as a minister in the Baptist Church. He was a brilliant and moving speaker and he soon became a leading figure in the campaign for equal rights for black Americans. In 1963, King made a famous speech in which he described his dream of a country where everyone was equal. He also helped to organize a march of 200,000 people on Washington DC to demand racial equality. Partly as a result of King's campaigns, the US government passed new laws on racial equality in 1964. King was assassinated in Memphis, Tennessee, in 1968.

Mother Teresa of Calcutta (1910–1997)

Mother Teresa was originally called Agnes Gonxha Bojaxhiu. She was born in Macedonia, but at the age of 18 she travelled to Ireland to join a convent of nuns who sent teachers to India. After a few months' training, she went to India and began work as a teacher in a Catholic school in Calcutta. Mother Teresa was a schoolteacher for 17 years, but in 1948, while she was on a train journey, she felt she heard the voice of God urging her to devote her life to helping the poor. She began to care for the poor, the sick and the dying in Calcutta and set up a school for the children of the slums. Many people came to help her in her work, and in 1950 she founded a new religious order, known as the Missionaries of Charity.

Archbishop Desmond Tutu (1931–)

Desmond Tutu was born in the Transvaal region of South Africa. He trained first as a teacher, and in 1960 he was ordained as an Anglican priest. In 1986, Tutu was made Archbishop of Cape Town. He was one of the leading figures in the struggle to end the apartheid system, in which black people were treated as second-class citizens. After apartheid was abolished in 1994, Archbishop Tutu worked to set up the Truth and Reconciliation Commission, in which those who committed injustices in the name of apartheid were given a fair hearing and then granted forgiveness. The commission was recognized as an outstanding example of Christian forgiveness.

Books

The Story of Christianity by Michael Collins and Matthew Price (Dorling Kindersley, 1999)
The Story of Christianity by Peter Partner (Andre Deutsch, 2005)
World Beliefs and Cultures: Christianity by Sue Penney (Heinemann Library, 2000)

Websites

www.bbc.co.uk/religion/religions/christianity/
A brief guide to Christianity, including sections on history, customs and holy days as well as news features on Christianity today

www.justus.anglican.org/resources/bio/
Very brief sketches of the lives of famous Christians

www.rejesus.co.uk/
A large website on the Christian religion, including interviews, prayers, and videos on the life of Christ

TIMELINE

c. 4   Birth of Jesus.

c. 27   Jesus gathers his disciples and starts to teach and perform miracles.

c. 33   Crucifixion of Jesus.

c. 35   Conversion of St Paul.

c. 46   St Paul sets off on the first of his three missionary journeys.

64   After the Great Fire of Rome, Emperor Nero starts to persecute Christians.

c. 65   St Mark completes his Gospel, the first of the Gospels of the New Testament.

303   Emperor Diocletian begins his great persecution of Christians.

305   The missionary Frumentius starts to convert the people of Ethiopia.

312   Emperor Constantine has a vision before the Battle of Milvian Bridge. After the battle, he encourages Christianity in the Roman Empire.

313   Constantine issues the Edict of Milan, allowing Christians in the empire to follow their religion.

325   Constantine holds the Council of Nicaea – the first of the great councils of the Church.

c. 350   St Basil establishes a set of rules for monks in the eastern Church.

391   Emperor Theodosius makes Christianity the official religion of the Roman Empire.

393   The New Testament is completed.

410   St Augustine of Hippo begins to write *The City of God*.

c. 440   St Patrick starts to convert Irish tribes.

c. 500   St Benedict establishes a community of monks. This is the start of the Benedictine order.

597   St Augustine starts to convert the Angles of southern England.

800   Pope Leo III crowns Charlemagne 'emperor of the Romans'.

909   The first Cluniac monastery is founded.

988   Russia becomes a Christian country.

1054   The Orthodox and Roman Catholic Churches split.

1095   Pope Urban II calls Christians to go on the First Crusade.

1098   St Bernard founds the Cistercian order.

1209   St Francis establishes the first order of Franciscan friars.

1215   St Dominic establishes a community of monks. This the start of the Dominican order.

1309   Pope Clement V moves from Rome to Avignon.

1517   Martin Luther posts his Ninety-five Theses on the church door in Wittenberg.

1520   Martin Luther is excommunicated. This is the start of Lutheranism.

1534   King Henry VIII announces that he is supreme head of the Church of England. This marks the start of Anglicanism.
St Ignatius Loyola founds the Jesuits.

1541   John Calvin establishes the Calvinist Church.

1545   The Council of Trent starts to meet. Meetings continue until 1563.

1560s   John Knox founds the Presbyterian Church in Scotland.

1612   The Separatists, later known as the Baptists, become established in England.

1618   The Thirty Years' War, between Catholics and Protestants, begins in Germany.

1620   The Pilgrims establish a colony in North America.

1650s   The Society of Friends is formed. Later the Friends become known as the Quakers.

1738   John Wesley begins to preach a new form of Christianity. This marks the start of Methodism.

1861   William Booth founds the Salvation Army.

1900s   The Pentecostal (or Charismatic) movement begins in Los Angeles, USA.

1948   The World Council of Churches is founded.

1964   The pope and the patriarch meet in a move to heal divisions between the Roman Catholic and Orthodox Churches.

1970s   The liberation theology movement begins in South America.

2000   Christians around the world celebrate two thousand years of Christianity.

FACTS AND FIGURES

Festivals and seasons

The main festivals and seasons of the Christian year are Advent, Christmas, Lent and Easter. Some festivals, such as Christmas Day, are celebrated on the same date every year. Others, such as Easter, change date slightly every year.

Month	Event	What happens
November/December	Advent	The season of Advent covers the four Sundays before Christmas. During Advent, Christians remember the coming of the Angel Gabriel to Mary and the events leading to the birth of Jesus.
December or January	Christmas	The festival of Christmas is held on 25 December in the Roman Catholic Church and 7 January in the Orthodox Church. On Christmas Day, Christians celebrate the birth of Jesus, often known as the Nativity.
February/March	Lent	The season of Lent is the 40-day period leading up to the Easter festival. During Lent, Christians remember Jesus' temptation in the wilderness and the events leading up to the Crucifixion of Jesus.
March or April	Easter	The festival of Easter lasts for three days, from Friday to Sunday. On Good Friday, Christians remember Christ's Crucifixion. On Easter Sunday, they celebrate his Resurrection.

Ceremonies

Two of the most important ceremonies in the Christian religion are baptism and Holy Communion.

Baptism Baptism is also known as christening. It is a ceremony to welcome a new member into the Christian faith. Some denominations baptize babies or children, while others baptize only adult Christians. In the baptism ceremony, new members come into contact with water – sometimes it is just poured over their head, and sometimes they are completely immersed in it. The immersion in water is a symbol of the person dying and being born again into the Christian faith.

Holy Communion Holy Communion is also known as the Eucharist and the Mass. It is a ceremony based on the Last Supper, which was held not long before the Crucifixion. At this meal, Jesus told his followers that the bread they were about to eat was his body and the wine they would drink was his blood. At Holy Communion, Christians eat bread and drink wine as a way of remembering Christ's death on the cross. The bread and blood are a symbol of the eternal life offered to Christians through Christ's death.

Saints' days

Each day of the Christian year is dedicated to the memory of a saint – a holy person who devoted his or her life to the Christian faith. Some of the best-known saints are:

St Valentine (14 February): St Valentine has become associated with love and romance.
St David (1 March): St David is the patron saint of Wales.
St Patrick (17 March): St Patrick is the patron saint of Ireland.
St George (23 April): St George is the patron saint of England.
St Andrew (30 November): St Andrew is the patron saint of Scotland.

Approximate numbers of Christians worldwide

1900	558,000,000
1985	1,000,000,000
1995	1,928,000,000
2005	2,100,000,000

Approximate numbers of Christians by continent (1995)

Africa	348,176,000
Asia	306,762,000
Europe	551,892,000
South America	448,006,000
North America	249,277,000
Oceania	23,840,000

GLOSSARY

abbot The leader of a group of monks.

amphitheatre A very large, circular stadium used for public entertainments.

Anglicans People who belong to the Church of England, a branch of the Christian Protestant movement. Anglicans are mainly found in England but there are branches of this Church all over the world.

Annunciation The Angel Gabriel's visit to the Virgin Mary, bringing the news that she would give birth to the Son of God.

apartheid The political system that used to operate in South Africa, in which black people were kept apart from whites and treated as second-class citizens.

apostles The followers of Christ who spread his message.

Baptists People who belong to the Baptist Church, a branch of the Christian Protestant movement. Baptists practise adult baptism.

barbarian The name the Romans gave to the tribes who lived outside the Roman Empire.

basilica A large church.

bishop A senior priest in the Christian Church. Bishops are in charge of all the priests and churches in a large area known as a diocese.

Calvinists People who belong to the Calvinist Church, a branch of the Christian Protestant movement. Calvinists believe in hell and damnation.

catacombs A series of tunnels under the city of Rome, where early Christians met to worship.

congregation A group of people gathered together for worship.

Congregationalists Members of the Congregationalist Church, a branch of the Christian Protestant movement. Congregationalists allow each congregation to manage its own church.

convent A group of buildings where nuns live and work.

creed A statement of what someone believes.

crucifixion The act of putting someone to death by fastening the person to a cross and leaving him or her there to die. In the Christian religion, the Crucifixion refers to Christ's death on the cross.

deacon A senior priest in the early Christian Church, who was in charge of practical matters, such as giving help to the poor.

denominations Branches or groups within the Christian Church.

disciples The twelve men chosen by Christ to be his followers.

ecumenical Aiming for unity and cooperation.

evangelism The taking of the Christian message out into the wider world.

excommunicated Expelled from the Roman Catholic Church.

friar A member of a Christian religious order who travels around, preaching and caring for the poor and sick.

heretic Someone who holds beliefs that contradict the Church's teachings.

hermit Someone who chooses to live totally alone and concentrate on God.

indulgences Pardons for sins, which were sold for money.

liberation theology A form of Christianity based on the belief that Christians have a duty to help the poor and the suffering.

Lutherans People who belong to the Lutheran Church, a branch of the Christian Protestant movement. Lutheran services are very simple and are based on readings from the Bible.

martyr Someone who is killed or is made to suffer because of his or her beliefs.

medieval To do with the Middle Ages, the period of history between approximately 1000 and 1450 CE.

meditation In Christianity, the practice of thinking very deeply about something.

Methodists People who belong to the Methodist Church, a branch of the Christian Protestant movement. Methodists hold simple services with rousing hymns and passionate sermons.

missionary Someone who travels to a foreign land to spread his or her beliefs.

monastery A group of buildings where monks live and work.

New Testament The second part of the Bible, which tells the life of Jesus and describes how his followers spread the Christian faith.

Nonconformists People who belong to any of the Protestant Churches, which are independent of the Roman Catholic Church.

ordain To make somebody into a priest in a special church service.

pagans People who worship their own gods and who do not belong to any of the main world religions.

Pentecostal Church A branch of the Christian Protestant movement. Pentecostal Christians hold very lively services, and some of their members claim to have the gifts of prophecy and healing. They are also sometimes known as Charismatic Christians.

pilgrimage A journey to worship at a holy place.

pope The head of the Roman Catholic Church.

Presbyterians People who belong to the Presbyterian Church, a branch of the Christian Protestant movement. Each congregation of the Presbyterian Church is governed by a group of elders.

prophecy Telling what will happen in the future.

Protestants Christians who do not belong to the Roman Catholic or Orthodox Churches.

Puritans Members of a Protestant Christian movement that developed in 16th-century England. The Puritans dressed very plainly and followed a simple form of worship.

Quakers Members of a Protestant Christian movement that developed in 17th-century England. Quakers gather in meeting houses rather than churches and they stress the importance of quiet meditation.

Resurrection Christ's coming back to life, three days after his death.

salvation The act of being saved from sin, so you can go to heaven.

scriptures Holy writings.

secular Not connected with religion.

shrine A holy building that often contains a sacred object, such as the remains of a saint.

temptations Offers of things you want, made in order to test you.

Virgin Mary The name Christians give to Mary, the mother of Jesus.

INDEX